FLORIDA PANTHERS

BY DAN SCIFO

Book design by Maggie Villaume
Cover design by Maggie Villaume

Photographs ©: Andy Clayton-King/AP Images, cover; Marta Lavandier/AP Images, 4–5, 10–11; Justin Tang/The Canadian Press/AP Images, 7; Frank Franklin II/AP Images, 8; Michael Caulfield/AP Images, 13; B. Bennett/Hulton Archive/Getty Images, 15; Hans Deryk/Rick Bowmer/AP Images, 16–17; Scott Martin/AP Images, 19; Gerald Herbert/AP Images, 20; Joel Auerbach/AP Images, 23; Alex Brandon/AP Images, 24–25, 27, 29

Press Box Books, an imprint of Press Room Editions.

ISBN
978-1-63494-594-3 (library bound)
978-1-63494-612-4 (paperback)
978-1-63494-647-6 (epub)
978-1-63494-630-8 (hosted ebook)

Library of Congress Control Number: 2022912843

Distributed by North Star Editions, Inc.
2297 Waters Drive
Mendota Heights, MN 55120
www.northstareditions.com

Printed in the United States of America
Mankato, MN
012023

ABOUT THE AUTHOR

Dan Scifo lives outside of Pittsburgh, Pennsylvania, with his wife and family. He has covered two Super Bowls, three Stanley Cup Finals, two NHL outdoor games, and two US Open golf championships throughout a career that spans more than 15 years as a sports journalist. He currently serves as a freelance correspondent for The Associated Press and USA Hockey.

TABLE OF CONTENTS

1

Sam Bennett posted a career-high 49 points in the 2021–22 season.

TOP CATS

The Florida Panthers' attack came fast and furious. It had been that way the entire 2021–22 season. Florida was on the way to its best regular season ever.

That all showed in a late April game against Ottawa. Early in the first period, Sam Bennett forced a turnover behind the Senators' net. Teammate Sam Reinhart got open at the bottom of the circle. Reinhart quickly shot Bennett's pass into the back of the net.

In the third period, another turnover helped the Panthers. This time Reinhart sent a long pass to Anthony Duclair. The Senators' goalie saved Duclair's one-timer. But Bennett tapped in a rebound from the top of the crease.

Just 21 seconds later, it was Carter Verhaeghe's turn. He raced up the ice with Eetu Luostarinen on a two-on-one. When Luostarinen sent a pass his way, Verhaeghe scored easily. Verhaeghe added another one later in the period. Maxim Mamin found the left winger

Carter Verhaeghe (left) celebrates with Eetu Luostarinen after scoring against the Ottawa Senators in an April 2022 game.

wide open at the side of the net. Verhaeghe couldn't miss from there.

The goal cemented a 4–0 shutout against the Senators. It was more than

Jonathan Huberdeau's 115 points were tied for the second-most in the NHL in 2021–22.

another win in the season, though. It clinched Florida's first Presidents' Trophy. That is awarded to the National Hockey League (NHL) team with the best record in the regular season. The Panthers' 58 wins and 122 points were both team records.

Florida scored in bunches to pile up those wins. The Panthers scored a team-record 337 goals. That was the most by any team since 1995–96. Of the team's 28 players, 13 set career highs in goals that season. Fourteen set career highs in assists and points. That included Jonathan Huberdeau. His 85 assists were the most in a season by a left winger in NHL history.

STREAKING CATS

The Panthers broke many team records in the 2021–22 season. They won 13 straight games from March 29 to April 23. It was the longest win streak in team history. That beat the 12-game win streak set during the 2015–16 season. The Panthers' attack was the main reason for the 13 wins. They scored 64 goals during the streak.

2

Ray Sheppard tallied 16 points in 21 games in the 1996 playoffs.

YEAR OF *THE RAT*

The NHL began in Canada. It later added teams in the United States. But its teams almost all played in cities with colder winters. The Panthers were part of changing that. The NHL began adding more southern cities during the 1990s. And in 1993–94, the league's newest team debuted in South Florida.

New teams usually struggle in their early years. The Panthers were good right away. They recorded the best debut season to that point for an NHL expansion team. By their third season, in 1995–96, they were in the playoffs.

That gave the hockey world an introduction to Florida's rat problem. The legend was born during the home opener. Right winger Scott Mellanby killed a rat in the Panthers' dressing room in the first intermission. He then scored two goals with the same stick. Goalie John Vanbiesbrouck called it a "Rat Trick."

BECOMING THE PANTHERS

Once Florida got a team, it needed a name. Team president Bill Torrey came up with the Panthers. The name honors the cougar species found in the swamps of the Sunshine State. Torrey had another reason. He hoped his team would play with the quickness and ferocity of a panther.

Scott Mellanby steals the puck from an opponent in a 1995 game against the Mighty Ducks of Anaheim.

Fans loved it. They began tossing rubber rats onto the ice to celebrate Florida goals.

Florida's first playoff series was against the Boston Bruins. The Panthers had a chance to win the series at home in Game 5. The game was tied 3–3 late in the third period. Then Bill Lindsay took over. The right winger zoomed past defenseman Ray Bourque. Out of desperation, Bourque tripped Lindsay. But it didn't stop him. Lindsay's goal sent Florida to the next round.

The Panthers beat the Philadelphia Flyers in six games. Next was the conference finals against the Pittsburgh Penguins. The Panthers went down 3–2 in the series. A 4–3 home win in Game 6 kept them alive. Penguins goalie Tom Barrasso hid in his net after a goal to avoid the rubber critters raining down from the fans. The Panthers then won Game 7.

Arena workers clean rubber rats off the ice during the 1996 Stanley Cup Final.

The run ended in the Stanley Cup Final. The Panthers were swept by the Colorado Avalanche. But fans would not soon forget the Year of the Rat.

3

John Vanbiesbrouck guards the net against the Pittsburgh Penguins in the 1996 playoffs.

DROUGHT IN *FLORIDA*

The Panthers reached the playoffs again in 1996–97. A big reason was goalie John Vanbiesbrouck. He was the foundation of the Panthers. Florida selected him with the first pick of the 1993 NHL Expansion Draft. Vanbiesbrouck won 106 games in a Florida uniform. He won 374 in his career. That was the most by a US-born goaltender when he retired in 2002.

A couple of down years followed 1997. Looking to reload, the Panthers traded for Pavel Bure in 1999. The Russian winger was one of the sport's most exciting players. By 2000, he had the Panthers back in the playoffs. His 58 goals that year led the NHL. Then he scored 59 goals in 2000–01. That led the league again.

However, all those goals didn't lead the Panthers to the playoffs. Starting in 2000–01, the Panthers went on to miss the playoffs for the next 10 seasons. Bad trades set the team back for years. One bright spot of this era was Roberto Luongo. The goalie turned out to be one of the most important players in team history. But he was traded to the Vancouver

Pavel Bure tallied 251 points in 223 games with the Panthers.

Olli Jokinen (12) congratulates Roberto Luongo after a shootout win in a 2006 game.

Canucks in 2006. It was another move that haunted the Panthers.

The 2000–01 season also saw the arrival of Olli Jokinen. The Finnish center got off to a slow start in Florida. But he tallied a team-high 65 points in the 2002–03 season. Jokinen was named team captain the next season. He kept that role until he was traded before the 2008–09 season. He left the Panthers with multiple team records. His six points in a 2007 game were the most by a Panther in one game. And he was Florida's all-time leader in goals with 188.

THE AGELESS JÁGR

Jaromír Jágr played 18 NHL seasons. Three were with the Panthers. He was in his 40s when he joined the team in February 2015. With the Panthers, Jágr passed Mark Messier for second all-time in career points. He also passed Brett Hull for third in career goals at the time. Jágr finished his career with 1,921 points. That put him second only to Wayne Gretzky.

ROBERTO LUONGO

The Panthers traded for Roberto Luongo during the 2000 NHL Draft. It turned out to be a great move for the Panthers. Luongo went on to set almost every goalie record in Florida. He became the team's leader in games played, wins, saves, and shutouts.

Luongo spent 11 seasons with the Panthers over two stints. In March 2020, the Panthers retired his number. It was the first number retired in team history.

Luongo was born in Montreal, Québec. But he said he considers Florida his home. He became an important member of the South Florida community. In 2018 there was a shooting at a local high school. The Panthers played a home game soon after. Luongo addressed the crowd. He said the teachers at the school were heroes. He added that the students gave him hope for the future.

Roberto Luongo played in 1,044 games, which ranks second among goalies in NHL history.

4

By his third season in 2015–16, Aleksander Barkov became a regular 20-goal scorer.

RECORD BREAKERS

The long stretch of losing gave the Panthers a lot of high draft picks. In 2011, Florida picked third. It selected forward Jonathan Huberdeau. In 2013, the Panthers got future captain Aleksander Barkov with the second pick. The following year, the Panthers picked defenseman Aaron Ekblad first overall.

All three of those players became stars. And it didn't take

long for a couple of them. In 2013, Huberdeau became the first Panther to win the Calder Memorial Trophy. That award is given to the NHL's best rookie each season. Ekblad won it in 2015.

Those players went on to make history. In 2020, Huberdeau recorded his 420th point. That passed Olli Jokinen for the team record. Barkov scored his

THE RATS RETURN

The rats invaded the ice once again. But this wasn't 1996 at the old Miami Arena. It was 2012 at BankAtlantic Center. The Panthers won their first division championship in team history during the 2011–12 season. Fans celebrated with the tradition started in 1996. Rubber rats hit the ice after the Panthers beat the New Jersey Devils in Game 2 of the first round. It was Florida's first playoff win since 1997.

Aaron Ekblad recorded 39 points as a rookie in the 2014–15 season.

189th career goal in 2021. That made him the leader for goals scored in team history.

In 2019, the Panthers signed goalie Sergei Bobrovsky. He was one of several

Panthers to have a historic 2021–22 season. Bobrovsky tied for the league lead with 39 wins. That also broke the team record set by Roberto Luongo.

The talented 2021–22 Panthers faced the Washington Capitals in the first round of the playoffs. The Panthers had a chance to win the series in Washington in Game 6. The game went to overtime after a late Capitals goal in the third period. However, Carter Verhaeghe scored early in overtime to send the Panthers to the next round. It was Florida's first playoff series win since 1996.

The Panthers were swept by the defending champion Tampa Bay Lightning in the next round. After the season, the

Carter Verhaeghe celebrates after his series-winning goal against the Washington Capitals in the 2022 playoffs.

Panthers traded Huberdeau to the Calgary Flames. They got young left winger Matthew Tkachuk in return. Fans hoped the team's young core could compete for years to come.

• FLORIDA PANTHERS QUICK STATS

FOUNDED: 1993

STANLEY CUP CHAMPIONSHIPS: 0

KEY COACHES:

- Doug MacLean (1996–1998), 83 wins, 71 losses, 33 ties
- Gerard Gallant (2015–2017), 96 wins, 65 losses, 25 overtime losses
- Andrew Brunette (2022–), 51 wins, 18 losses, 6 overtime losses

HOME ARENA: FLA Live Arena (Sunrise, FL)

MOST CAREER POINTS: Jonathan Huberdeau (613)

MOST CAREER GOALS: Aleksander Barkov (220)

MOST CAREER ASSISTS: Jonathan Huberdeau (415)

MOST CAREER SHUTOUTS: Roberto Luongo (38)

**Stats are accurate through the 2021–22 season.*

GLOSSARY

CAPTAIN
A team's leader.

CREASE
The area directly in front of the goalie, painted in blue.

EXPANSION
The way leagues grow by adding new teams.

ONE-TIMER
A shot taken by a player who both receives a pass and shoots the puck all in one motion.

REBOUND
When the goalie makes the save, but the puck goes back into play.

TRADITION
A custom or belief that is passed down from generation to generation.

TO LEARN MORE

BOOKS

Davidson, B. Keith. *NHL*. New York: Crabtree Publishing, 2022.

Graves, Will. *Pro Hockey Upsets*. Minneapolis: Lerner Publications, 2020.

Hewson, Anthony K. *GOATs of Hockey*. Minneapolis: Abdo Publishing, 2022.

MORE INFORMATION

To learn more about the Florida Panthers, go to **pressboxbooks.com/AllAccess**.

These links are routinely monitored and updated to provide the most current information available.

INDEX